Staying Dry

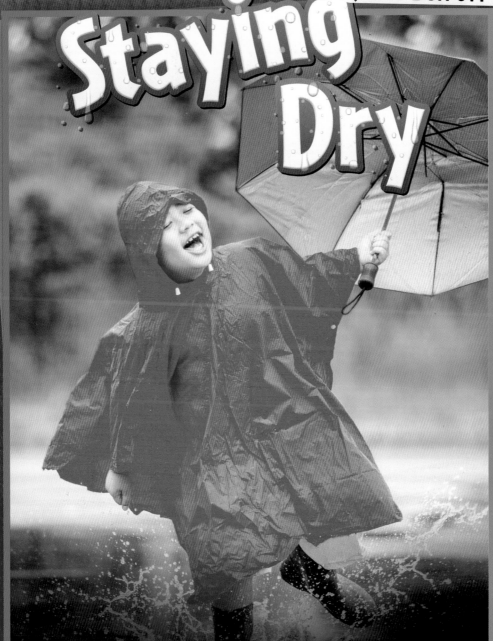

Heather E. Schwartz

✳ Smithsonian

Contributing Author

Jennifer Lawson

Consultants

Madelyn Shaw
Curator
National Museum of American History

Sharon Banks
3rd Grade Teacher
Duncan Public Schools

Publishing Credits

Rachelle Cracchiolo, M.S.Ed., *Publisher*
Conni Medina, M.A.Ed., *Managing Editor*
Diana Kenney, M.A.Ed., NBCT, *Content Director*
Véronique Bos, *Creative Director*
Robin Erickson, *Art Director*
Michelle Jovin, M.A., *Associate Editor*
Mindy Duits, *Senior Graphic Designer*
Smithsonian Science Education Center

Image Credits: p.8 Rebecca Cole/Alamy; p.13 Volker Steger/Science Source; p.14 (bottom) Juniors Bildarchiv GmbH/Alamy; pp.14–15 Robert Harding/Alamy; p.15 (bottom) Tim Nowack/National Geographic; p.23 (bottom left) Mark Bowler/Science Source; p.23 (bottom right) E. R. Degginger/Science Source; p.24 (bottom) © Smithsonian; p.25 (top) Dr Jeremy Burgess/Science Source; all other images from iStock and/or Shutterstock.

Library of Congress Cataloging-in-Publication Data
Names: Schwartz, Heather E., author.
Title: Staying dry / Heather E. Schwartz.
Description: Huntington Beach, CA : Teacher Created Materials, [2019] | Includes index. | Audience: K to grade 3. |
Identifiers: LCCN 2018030488 (print) | LCCN 2018036679 (ebook) | ISBN 9781493869121 | ISBN 9781493866724
Subjects: LCSH: Rain and rainfall--Juvenile literature. | Waterproof clothing--Juvenile literature.
Classification: LCC QC924.7 (ebook) | LCC QC924.7 .S35 2019 (print) | DDC 677/.682--dc23
LC record available at https://lccn.loc.gov/2018030488

Smithsonian

© 2019 Smithsonian Institution. The name "Smithsonian" and the Smithsonian logo are registered trademarks owned by the Smithsonian Institution.

Teacher Created Materials

5301 Oceanus Drive
Huntington Beach, CA 92649-1030
www.tcmpub.com
ISBN 978-1-4938-6672-4
© 2019 Teacher Created Materials, Inc.
Printed in Malaysia
Thumbprints.21251

Table of Contents

3

Rainy Days

Imagine that you are about to leave on a trip. The weather **forecast** says it will rain. Luckily, you have a lot of rain gear. It will help keep you dry. It is all waterproof, so the rain will not get on your skin.

Why do we need to stay dry? How is rain gear made? And how is it **inspired** by nature? It all starts with wet weather.

THE WEATHER FORECAST

MON	TUE	WED	THU	FRI
RAIN	RAIN	RAIN	RAIN	RAIN
63	61	62	60	61

LIVE

8:15 AM ▶ RAIN IS IN THE FORECAST. WEAR RAIN GEAR TO STAY DRY.

Wet Weather

The water cycle starts when heat from the sun warms water. When water gets very hot, it turns into a gas. This is called evaporation. The gas it becomes is called water vapor (VAY-puhr).

Water vapor rises into the air. It cools as it rises. Once it is cool enough, it makes clouds. This is called condensation.

Clouds cool too. Once clouds get very cold, liquid water forms once more. Water falls from the clouds as freezing rain, sleet, hail, or snow. Those are all types of precipitation. Then, the water cycle starts all over!

Water vapor rises from a hot spring in Yellowstone National Park.

The Water Cycle

A red squirrel shakes off water to stay dry.

Playing in water can be fun. It feels great when the weather is hot. So, what is the big deal about staying dry?

Humans need to stay dry most of the time. Staying dry means staying warm. People lose **body heat** in water. Also, human skin is not designed to stay wet for days at a time.

This bumblebee got wet in the rain.

Being a Bee

Rain can keep animals from doing what they do best. For example, bees cannot fly in heavy rain. The rain pushes them off course. Rain clouds can also block the sun, which bees use to find their way.

A brother and sister play in the sprinklers on a hot day.

People lose body heat up to 25 times faster in cold water than they do in cold air.

Water can also ruin people's things. For instance, what might happen if someone left a drawing out in the rain? The water would cause the colors to run. It would soak the paper. It would make the paper tear. People do not just want to keep themselves dry during a downpour. They want to keep their stuff dry too.

This photographer uses an umbrella to keep their camera dry.

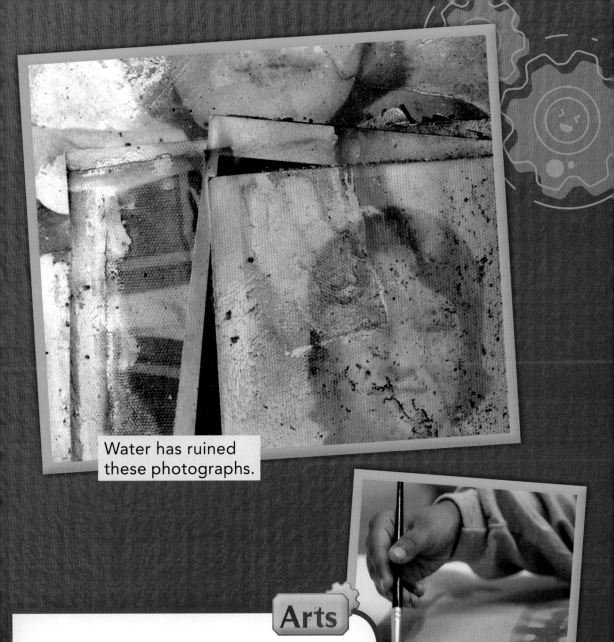

Water has ruined these photographs.

Painting with Water

Watercolor paints are made of water and **pigment**. They also have a "binder." The binder helps the paint stick to the paper. These paints can be used to create detailed paintings.

Some engineers study plants for ideas on staying dry.

Staying dry in wet weather takes work. But these days, it is easier than ever. There are raincoats and rain boots. There are umbrellas too. Rain may fall. But people can stay dry.

People have **engineers** to thank for rain gear. Engineers find ways to make things better. They sometimes look at nature for ideas. That is where the best designs are often found.

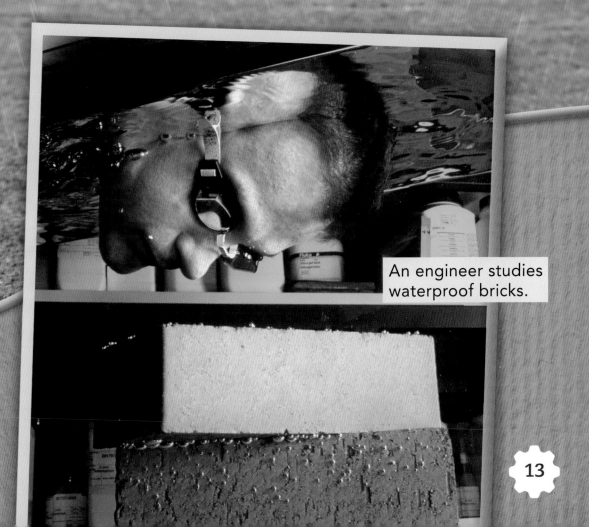

An engineer studies waterproof bricks.

Natural Protection

Wet weather is a fact of life. Animals know where to go to stay dry. Some animals look down. They dig tunnels in the ground to stay away from rain. Other animals find plants to use as shelter. Leaves can block rainfall.

Engineers see how animals stay dry. It inspires them to keep people dry the same way.

A pygmy rabbit uses a leaf as shelter from the rain.

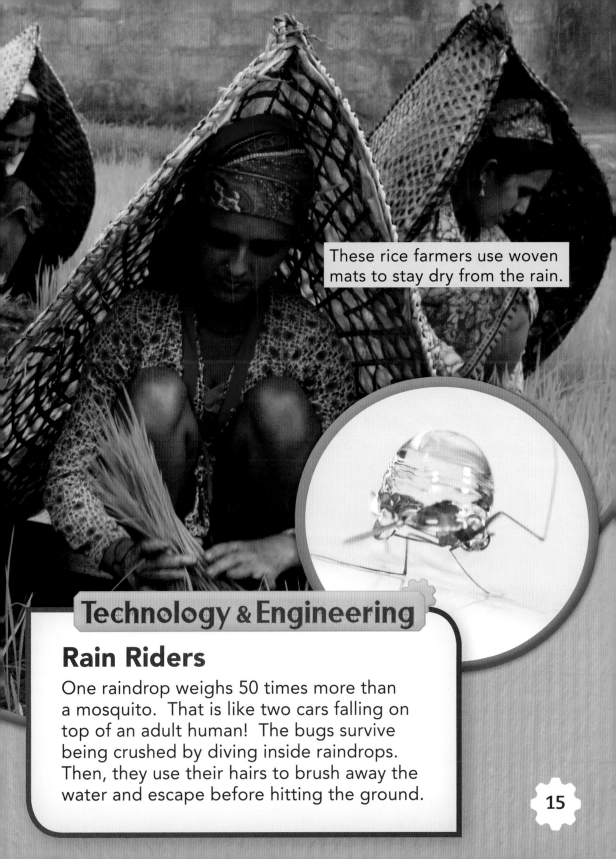

These rice farmers use woven mats to stay dry from the rain.

Technology & Engineering

Rain Riders

One raindrop weighs 50 times more than a mosquito. That is like two cars falling on top of an adult human! The bugs survive being crushed by diving inside raindrops. Then, they use their hairs to brush away the water and escape before hitting the ground.

Many engineers look to reptiles for ideas. Reptiles' skin is made of **keratin**. It is the same substance as human nails. Keratin makes things waterproof. Keratin does not wash off in the rain, either.

Engineers make rain gear that is like keratin. The gear keeps things dry. And the gear does not wash off in the rain.

The keratin on this alligator's skin makes it waterproof.

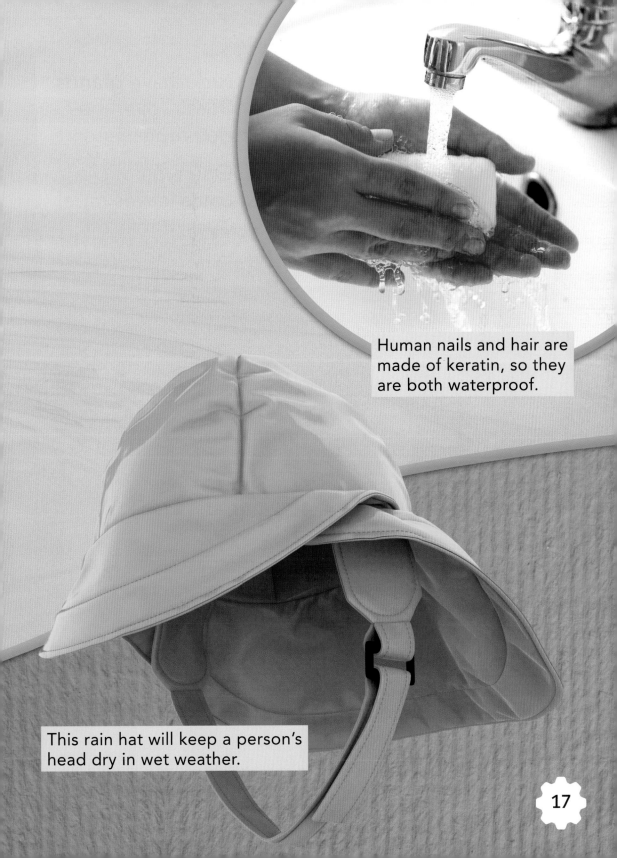

Human nails and hair are made of keratin, so they are both waterproof.

This rain hat will keep a person's head dry in wet weather.

Engineers study ducks too. Ducks have **glands** on their bodies that make oil. Ducks cover their feathers with this oil. The oil helps **repel** water.

Engineers also study plants. One type of plant they look at is the lotus plant. Lotus leaves repel water. When water hits lotus leaves, it rolls off. The leaves stay dry.

Baby ducks cannot make oil and are not waterproof. Instead, mother ducks spread oil on their ducklings.

Lotus leaves stay dry, even in wet weather.

lotus flower

Inspired Inventions

Engineers have learned ways to keep people dry. They know they can **coat** things with chemicals. This can make things waterproof. But some chemicals are **toxic**. They are not safe.

Instead, engineers have found a safer way. They have made a new kind of coating. It acts like lotus leaves. It can be used on clothes and boots to make them repel water.

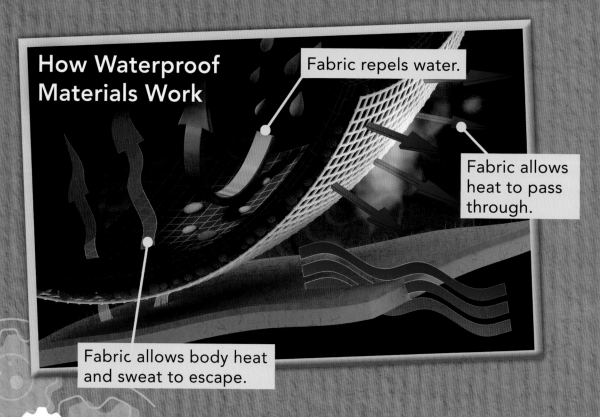

How Waterproof Materials Work

Fabric repels water.

Fabric allows heat to pass through.

Fabric allows body heat and sweat to escape.

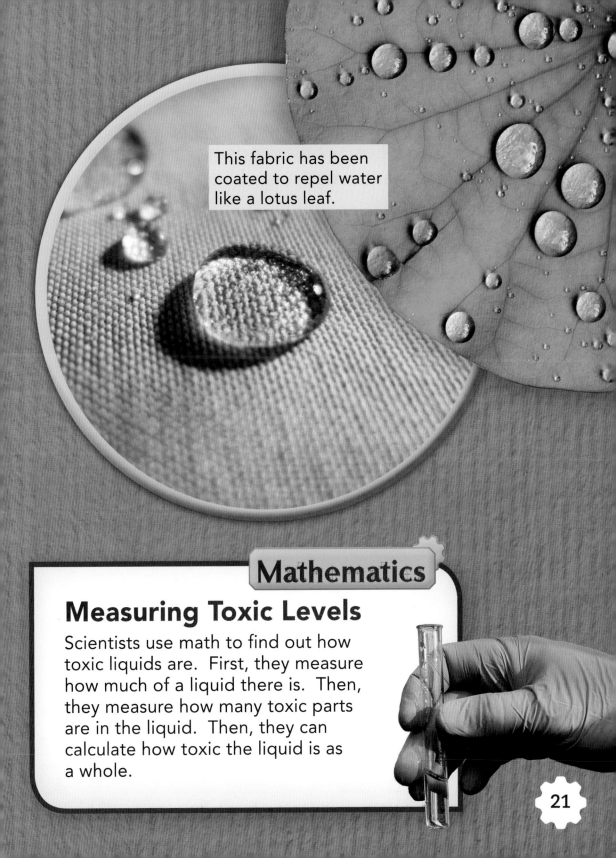

This fabric has been coated to repel water like a lotus leaf.

Measuring Toxic Levels

Scientists use math to find out how toxic liquids are. First, they measure how much of a liquid there is. Then, they measure how many toxic parts are in the liquid. Then, they can calculate how toxic the liquid is as a whole.

Based on Butterflies

Engineers have also made gear based on morpho butterflies. Their wings have patterns. The patterns have small raised lines. These lines are called ridges.

Ridges help repel rain. Water bounces off the ridges. That helps keep morpho butterflies' wings dry. Drops of water barely touch the wings. Then, they quickly bounce off again. Gear based on these wings works fast too.

A blue morpho butterfly prepares to fly.

blue morpho
butterfly

wing pattern

ridges

Working with Whales

People haven't always had high-tech gear to wear in the rain. Ancient hunters wore clothes made of whale and seal **intestines**. Rain could not get through. But sweat could get out. It worked great as rain gear.

Engineers copied this design. They made a fabric called Gore-Tex®. It keeps rain out. But it lets water vapor (as sweat) escape. It keeps people dry in rain, even when they sweat.

This raincoat was made of whale intestines by the Unangax people of Alaska.

This close-up photo shows the layers of Gore-Tex fabric.

These boots are made with Gore-Tex.

Rain Gear Really Works

Waterproof gear is important. It keeps people dry and warm. It takes a lot of hard work to make that gear. And engineers are still learning more. They look at nature for answers.

You can find answers in nature too. The next time it rains, look outside. Notice how nature stays safe from rain. Study it like an engineer. You, too, can help people stay dry.

These friends watch a snail crawl on the wet ground while they stay warm and dry.

STEAM CHALLENGE

Define the Problem

It is supposed to be a very rainy winter this year. A store has hired you to make a piece of winter clothing to sell. Your clothing should be waterproof and strong.

  Constraints: You may use no more than five items.

Criteria: Your clothing must fit a friend. Your friend must stay dry when 250 milliliters (1 cup) of water is poured onto the clothing.

Research and Brainstorm

Why is it important for humans to stay dry? What are some ways that plants and animals are "waterproof"?

Design and Build

Sketch a plan of your clothing. What purpose will each part serve? What materials will work best? Build the model.

Test and Improve

Have a friend wear your clothing outside. Pour 250 mL (1 c.) of water onto the clothing. Did your friend stay dry? How can you improve your clothing? Improve your design and try again.

Reflect and Share

In what other ways can you test your design? Will your design work in the snow? Are there any other materials you can use to make your design more successful?

Glossary

body heat—heat that is made in the body of a living human or animal

coat—cover with a thin layer

engineers—people who use science to design solutions for problems or needs

forecast—a statement about what will happen in the future

glands—organs in the body that make substances to be used by the body

inspired—given an idea about what to do or make

intestines—long tubes in the body that help break down food after it leaves the stomach

keratin—a shield-like part of hair, nails, and skin

pigment—a substance that gives color to other materials

repel—to keep something away or out

toxic—containing a harmful, poisonous substance

Index

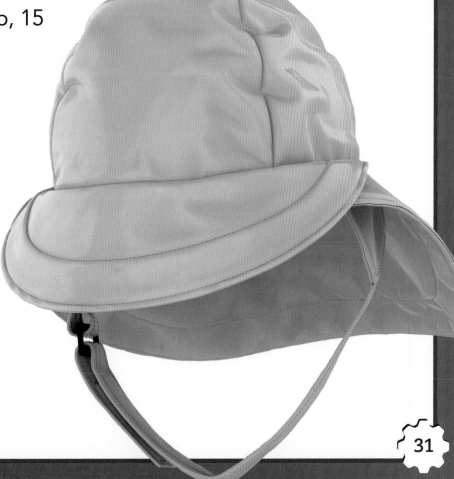

Career Advice
from Smithsonian

Do you want to help people stay dry? Here are some tips to get you started.

"Study the history and science of fabric. Maybe you will invent a new fabric that keeps people even drier." —*Tim Winkle, Curator*

"In college, study engineering and art to learn about design. Also study animals, such as sheep, and plants, such as cotton, to learn how they stay dry." —*Madelyn Shaw, Curator*